Copyı

Hauser Publishing Inc.

Los Angeles

www.hauserpub.com

Hauser
Publishing

Pictures: Courtesy of Nicole Spohn

Cover Design: Enrique Almeida

ISBN-10: 1-939534-34-8

ISBN-13: 978-1-939534-34-7

INTRODUCTION.........................1

Getting there 4

The Climate: Why it's ideal?..........6

ATTRACTIONS.........................8

Vineyards..........................8

Tecaté Area........................8

Cava Garcia........................8

Good to know.......................10

Vinos Tanama.......................11

Vinedos Don Juan...................12

Fiesta de la Vendemia..............13

Central Valley.....................14

San Antonio Nécua..................14

L.A. Cetto.........................14

La Casa De Doña Lupe...............16

Casa Pedro Domecq..................18

Accommodations: Where to
stay in Valle De Guadalupe.........19

Paralelo...........................23

Viñedos Lafarga....................25

Fancisco Zarco Area & the Southern Valle De Guadalupe.................26

    Lechuza Vinicola.................26

    Mogor Badan.................27

    Editor's Pick: Deckman's en el Mogor....28

    Viñas De Garza.................29

    Sol Y Barro.................30

    Vinacola Tres Mujeres & El Pinar De Tres Mujeres.................31

San Antonio De Las Minas.................33

    Viña de Liceaga.................33

    Casa de Piedra.................34

    Vinacola Tres Valles.................35

    Vinisterra.................36

    Santo Tomas.................37

El Sauzal & the Western Valle De Guadalupe.................38

    Cavas Valmar.................38

    Relieve Vinicola & Mixtura.................39

    AlXimia.................40

    Vinos Pijoan.................41

    Hacienda La Lomita.................42

    Vena Cava.................43

Villa Montefiori............................44

Vinos Bibayoff............................45

El Porvenier Area............................46

Finca la Carrodilla............................46

El Cielo............................47

Las Nubes............................48

J.C. Bravo............................49

Emeve............................50

Barón Balch'é............................51

Vinicola Torres Alegre............................52

Quinta Monasterio............................53

Shimul............................54

Vinos Suenoz............................55

Vinos Fuentes............................56

Monte Xanic............................57

Chateau Camou............................58

Francisco Zarco Area............................59

Vinedos Malagón............................59

Tintos del Norte 32............................60

Restaurants............................61

Museums & Other Cultural Institutions.....65

Museo de la Vid y el Vino............................65

La Escuelita............................66

Off the Beaten Path: Rancho Cortes..................................69

Off the Beaten Path: San Antonio Necua..................................70

Introduction

Mexico's Valle de Guadalupe is often referred to as the new Napa. But a tour of its wineries, hotels and restaurants shows that it's much more than that; it's very much its own place. The unique flavors of the region, the peaceful scenery, the warm hearted people allowed Baja's wine country to develop its very own identity. The region is standing its ground and, lately, offers more well known competitor's across the border a run for their money.

While tourism is definitely on the rise in the Valle De Guadalupe, the numbers are still small enough to allow for a sense of discovery. Country lanes off La Ruta del Vino, the main highway cutting through the valley and connecting Tecaté in the north and Ensenada in the south, lead to unexpected, hidden haciendas, architecturally striking wineries and alfresco eateries with soul-stirring views. Baja's wine region is so untouched, so romantic you almost don't want to tell people about it, just to keep it the way it is.

Valle De Guadalupe is a place of green valleys, calming lavender fields and boulder-covered hills, where it's not unusual that you will find churros, Mexican cowboys, riding along the newly paved highway or quaint casitas with no electricity located right next door to luxury ranches. Paired with the deep blue Baja sky, it feels like you are sipping wine from inside a landscape painting.

The legend behind the birth of the Mexican wine industry is that the Spanish Conquistador Hernán Cortés and his men exhausted their wine supply after celebrating the conquest of the Aztecs in the 16th century. In order to abbey their thirst, the Spaniards demanded recipients of land grants to plant vines in the hopes of soon replenishing their stock.

As an industry though, the Mexican wine production is still in its infamy, with bottles rarely being found outside of Mexico and only the largest wineries exporting to the U.S. In fact, the modern era of winemaking didn't start until some 20 years ago, when Hugo D'Acosta, a Bordeaux educated native of Mexico City, arrived in the Valle De Guadalupe and founded his flagship winery, Casa de Piedra.

As it's quite common for young wine regions, many local wine producers in the Valle De Guadalupe are taking an experimental approach to the craft. Of course you can't get grapes like Pinot Noir or Gewürztraminer to grow in the rigid Baja terrain; those delicate grapes simply won't grow in this harsh environment. But you will find everything from Malbec to Cabs to Chardonnay.

The Nebbiolo grape of the Piedmont region of Italy is growing to become the signature grape of Baja, although it may seem like a rather unlikely choice in a wine region where the temperature can easily exceed 110 degrees. In a recent interview series featuring Baja vinters, Paolo Paoloni, an Italian winemaker who's been in the Valle De Guadalupe since 1997, explained that the region's grapes produce wines darker, heavier and bolder in tannins than in their natural habitat, adding a unique touch to Valle De Guadalupe's Nebbiolo.

Tempranillo, the dominant red grape of Spain, is also widely planted throughout the Valle De Guadalupe and seems a more plausible solution, given the arid conditions of the valley which more closely resemble the climate of the grape-growing parts of Spain than that of Northern Italy.

The following chapters will detail how Baja's vintners learned to work with the very unique conditions they found in the Valle de Guadalupe, describe the products they developed and the methods they chose to make the region one of the top travel destinations for wine lovers.

Unlike the many wine and travel blogs you will find featuring posts about the Valle De Guadalupe and the rise of the Mexican wine region as the new Napa, this book doesn't highlight a few vineyards; it features a comprehensive list of wineries, restaurants, hotels and things to do – all listed by region, allowing visitors to plan their trip depending on where they may stay. Thus What To Do In The Valle De Guadalupe enables you to get the most out of your time spent in Baja's wine country, no matter how long you decide to stay.

Getting there

Valle De Guadalupe is located just a short drive inland from Ensenada. It straddles carretera federal 3, Highway 3, which connects Ensenada and Tecaté and can be accessed from either the north or the south.

If you are coming from the San Ysidro border crossing, you will be passing through Rosarito before you get to the turnoff located in the town of El Sauzal, just a few miles north of Ensenada. The road leading to the turnoff is a toll road. This is the only way it can be maintained, as it runs along the San Andreas fault and has to be worked on on a consistent basis. Pesos as well as Dollars are accepted as toll. Credit cards are not accepted.

If you want to avoid paying toll, access Highway 3 from Tecaté. The border town marks the northern access point of the highway. From the crossing, simply follow Avenida Universidad through town. It will automatically drop you onto Carretera Federal 3, Highway 3.

Highway 3 has recently been marked as Ruta del Vino, a name it was given by the local tourist board to attract visitors to the area. The 47-mile/76-kilometer long Wine Route connects more than 60 wineries in a 35-square-mile radius, some are easier to spot than others.

If you are looking for a particular winery, keep an eye out on the kilometer markers on the side of the road, as most addresses in the Valle De Guadalupe are referring to the kilometer count. Example: If an address reads, km. 7.5 Carretera Federal #3, it means that the entrance to the winery is located about halfway between kilometer marker 7 and kilometer marker 8.

There are plenty of wineries and restaurants located just off the main road; an even larger amount can be accessed via various dirt roads. After a rare rainy day, this may require an all-wheel-drive-vehicle.

The Climate: Why it's ideal?

Baja California's dry, hot summers and cooler, damper winters, combined with porous soil and cooling sea breezes, are ideal for grape growing. The northern end of the Baja California peninsula is, in fact, one of the New World's oldest wine growing regions. Jesuit priests cultivated vines here as early as the 18th century. The first commercial winery, Bodegas de Santo Tomas, opened in 1888.

The wines of the Baja region have always been known as really big, really bold – with lots of flavors. But it wasn't until Wall Street Journal wine critic Lettie Teague visited the Valle De Guadalupe in 2014 and openly critiqued the salty characteristics of the, as she put it, "far from thrilling" wines, that a discussion about the salinity of Baja's wines was initiated.

The one and only Valle De Guadalupe wine that critic Teague held up as an example of a quality seems to be the most technically advanced one, the El Mogor blend. It's best described as a wine that might as well come from Napa.

But is the wine which is perhaps the least representative of the region really the best? Or does the boldness and spiciness of Baja wine express something that's unique and should be embraced instead of critiqued?

Only time will tell. Maybe Teague's article is really just another example of the homogenization of Western critical thought. Are we possibly looking for wines that share a sameness?

"Wine tends to be really a territorial thing", as Israel Zenteno, the plant manager at Monte Xanic points out in the eBook *Conversations With Winemakers*. "It grows from a land and it grows differently in every land in the world, so it's a good representation of what your land is like". Or as fellow Valle De Guadalupe winemaker Pau Pijoan of Viñas Pijoan likes to put it: If kept in check, the salinity can add to the character of the wine.

Attractions

Vineyards

Tecaté Area

Cava Garcia

If you are entering the wine route from Tecaté in the north, Cava Garcia is the first winery you will reach. It's located just a few steps to the east of Highway 3 and can easily be accessed by car.

Although one of the younger vineyards in the area, wine making has a long tradition in the Garcia family. Winemaker Pedro Garcia's family imported the first grapes from Spain in 1950 and has been involved in the industry ever since.

Today, the Garcia family grows Zinfandel, Grenache and a lesser known grape called Rosa de Peru, which was brought to the Valle De Guadalupe by Russian emigrants in the early 20th century.

You can usually find a lot of locals at Cava Garcia, and once you walk in the tasting room, you will immediately understand why. It's a rustic but warm atmosphere with wooden benches and wine barrels that serve as decoration. With owner Pedro Garcia often greeting guests himself, you will immediately feel welcome.

Besides wine, goat cheese and olive oil, Cava Garcia also sells custom furniture made of white oak barrels.

The nearby Farm Cava is home to a variety of animals such as birds, donkeys, emus, horses, ponies and goats.

On a footnote: Cava Garcia serves the reds slightly chilled, as that is how the locals like them.

Cava Garica, *Km. 3 Carretera Federal #3 Tecaté-Ensenada, Phone: (665)799-6175*

Good to know...

Most tasting rooms are open on weekends. Should you be traveling during the week or over the holidays and have a particular winery in mind you wish to visit, it's advisable to call beforehand and check on the opening hours. You may even wish to set up an appointment. The same applies to the many restaurants in the area.

Vinos Tanama

Vinos Tanama, located just south of Cava Garica on the west side of the highway, is known as the "rising star of Tecaté". With a limited annual production, Tanama wines are highly sought after. All aged in oak barrels, the winery produces Cabernet Sauvignon, Rosé and a unique Tempranillo-Cabernet blend called Californio.

Formal production at Vinos Tanama didn't begin until the year 2000, but the winery is the descendant of more than 100 years of winemaking in the Valle De Guadalupe. Tanama is an ancient word from the language of the Kumiai tribe meaning "place of fertile land, where the water flows and oak trees grow". The name was chosen by founder Ricardo Gonzalez to represent the lush land and rolling fields of grape vines when he purchased this gorgeous tract of land just south of Tecaté in 1945 and began nurturing it. In 1999, his son learned that the local L.A. Cetto winery had canceled their contract with the vineyard. It was then, when the Gonzalez family decided to develop their own boutique label, Vinos Tanama.

The vineyards of the Gonzalez family are tucked away in the beautiful Valle Tanama, which is filled with expansive ranchos and tasteful haciendas. Tours of the winery and wine tastings as well as horseback tours of the valley are offered. Please call ahead for tour times or to set up an appointment.

Vinos Tanama, km. 7.5 Carretera Federal #3 Tecaté-Ensenada, Phone: (664) 215- 9090, Website: http://www.vinostanama.com.mx

Vinedos Don Juan

Located in the picturesque Valle de las Palmas about 20 miles / 32 kilometers south of Tecaté, Vinedos Don Juan is a small family-run winery. The founder, which is known among his friends as "Don Juan", has not only been an active member of the wine industry in the state of Baja California for the past 20 years, he's also a pioneer when it comes to implementing environmentally safe practices in the area. Every year, a new green initiative is adopted at his winery, reaching from carbon-neutral, chlorine free labels to recycled bottles. Vinedos Don Juan is a true green vineyard.

Thanks to the mineral rich soil and the arid climate of the Valle de las Palmas vineyards, Don Juan's wines have won many awards. This includes recognition at Valle De Guadalupe's annual Fiesta de la Vendemia, where Don Juan's Cabernet Sauvignon and Syrah took silver medals.

A third type of wine, which is produced at Vinedos Don Juan, is the little more experimental Meritage. It's a unique blend of Cabernet Sauvignon, Merlot and Syrah.

Vinedos Don Juan offers tastings and tours and also features an on-site store called **La Esperanza**, which retails locally grown products including honey, homemade preserves and olive oil.

Vinedos Don Juan, km. 28 Carretera Federal #3 Tecaté - Ensenada, Phone: (664) 681-1386 or (661) 681-6112, Website: http://www.vinedosdonjuan.com

Fiesta de la Vendemia

Each August, the Valle de Guadalupe wineries celebrate their harvest with a food and wine festival called Fiesta de la Vendemia, the Harvest Festival. Over the course of two weeks, various events take place at rotating wineries in the Guadalupe Valley as well as in the nearby coastal town of Ensenada. The schedule is usually released month in advance and can be found on the festival's website.

Harvest time is the busiest season in the Valle De Guadalupe. Tickets for the various events need to be purchased well in advance and hotel reservations should be made as soon as the dates are released.

Fiesta de la Vendemia, Phone: (646) 174-0170, Website: http://fiestasdelavendimia.com

Central Valley

San Antonio Nécua

L.A. Cetto

The most famous among the wineries in Valle De Guadalupe, L.A. Cetto produces approximately 1,000,000 cases of wine each year in three facilities. It's the largest wine producer in Mexico and one of the largest wineries in all of Latin America; L.A. Cetto even exports wines to the US, a rarity among the wineries in Valle De Guadalupe.

Although operating internationally and with tasting rooms in multiple cities, L.A. Cetto prides itself as a family-run business. It's headed by Luis Alberto, a third generation Cetto in the Valle De Guadalupe. Lured by the beautiful terrain and ideal growing conditions he found in the area, his grandfather left his native Italy in 1926 with the goal of bringing Mediterranean wine production to Mexico.

Today, L.A. Cetto produces the largest variety of wines among the vineyards in Valle De Guadalupe. The winery's extensive collection includes Cabernet Sauvignon, Chardonnay, Chenin Blanc, Nebbiolo, Petite Sirah, Vinifera wines, Zinfandel and exclusive reserves such as Champbrule Brut, Sangiovese and Viognier. Even Brandy and Tequila are produced on the premises.

With the growing popularity of the Valle De Guadalupe, cruise ships docking in Ensenada started shuttling passengers to the L.A. Cetto winery. Their spacious tasting room can handle the crowds, allowing guests to simply stroll in without a reservation. Tours of the winery's airplane hangar sized production facility are offered in English and Spanish and allow a behind-the-scenes look at fermentation, the aging of new wines in French oak barrels and the bottling process.

Integrating their passion for wine with a sincere appreciation of food, entertainment and artistry, L.A. Cetto frequently sponsors unique events at the winery's amphitheater such as the Festival de la Paella y El Vino, Mariachi Vargas and of course the much beloved annual grape harvest celebration, Fiesta de la Vendimia, which celebrates Valle de Guadalupe's rich, thriving community of winemakers, artisans, artists and enthusiasts.

L.A. Cetto is also home to one of the most popular picnic areas in the entire Valle De Guadalupe. Overlooking the vineyards and valley below, the romantic location has been the site of many marriage proposals.

Inspired by the view but forgot your picnic basket? Not a problem at all, simply visit the winery's boutique store to purchase cheese, crackers and olive oil produced on-site from olive trees that shield the delicate vines from the wind.

L.A. Cetto, km 73.5 Carretera Federal #3 Tecaté - Ensenada, Phone: (646) 155-2179, Website: http://www.cettowines.com

La Casa De Doña Lupe

Located just south of the famous L.A. Cetto is the more serene and intimate La Casa De Doña Lupe, a true gem among the wineries in Valle de Guadalupe. The winery is run by Doña Lupe and her son Daniel. Born in Sonora Badesi, Doña Lupe attended primary school only through fifth grade. But that hasn't stopped her from developing the 30 hectares of land purchased by her late husband into the poster child of the organic wine and food movement in Valle De Guadalupe.

At La Casa De Doña Lupe no chemical fertilizers, herbicides or pesticides are used. Even when the crops were attacked by the notorious olive fruit fly, Doña Lupe's son Daniel, who studied to become an organic vintner, chose to use neem-based products rather than jumping on board with the dimethoate used by other less holistic wineries in the region.

The holistic approach at the Doña Lupe winery has resulted in vibrant, flavorful crops, which are essential to the beloved desert wines La Casa De Doña Lupe has become known for. These include the Grenache-Sauvignon Blanc blend Senorita. Other delightful wine options include Doña Lupe's honey wine as well as a wine made from raisined grapes.

Wine connoisseurs who prefer a dryer, bolder flavor will appreciate the Ruby Cabernet/Cabernet blend and one of Doña Lupe's newer additions, the Nebbiolo/Cabernet Sauvignon blend.

At Casa De Doña Lupe, all wines are served in a Spanish style tasting room with homemade pizza, which is freshly prepared by Doña Lupe's daughter, Shirley, who has recently returned to the farm. She runs the adjacent small store, where you can purchase the family's homemade jams, sauces, olive oil, bread, cheese as well as Doña

Lupe's flavored tequila, which is a favorite among locals and tourists alike.

Even though La Casa De Doña Lupe is quickly making itself a name among the wineries in the Valle De Guadalupe, please don't expect large crowds. The Doña Lupe family farm and winery are very low key, and the family is determined to keep it that way. There are no plans to expand production and no attempts to capture a larger space within the international market. La Casa de Doña Lupe is happy to be a family business with all of the integrity and autonomy that comes with it. And you will be able to tell, once you set your first step on the property. At La Casa de Doña Lupe you will feel at home right away.

La Casa De Doña Lupe, km 73.5 Carretera Federal #3 Tecaté - Ensenada, Phone: (646) 155-2323, Website: http://www.lacasadonalupe.com

Casa Pedro Domecq

Located not far from what has become the most photographed hotel in Valle De Guadalupe, the modern Encuentro Guadalupe, is Casa Pedro Domecq. Established in 1972, Domecq, as it's often referred to by locals, was the first commercial winery, which was established in Valle De Guadalupe.

Today, Casa Pedro Domecq is the second largest wine producer in Mexico after L.A. Cetto and owned by the same company that produces El Presidente Brandy and Absolute Vodka. Several of Domecq's most beloved labels such as Calafia and Padre Xino are produced in the Valle de Guadalupe and can be enjoyed in the tasting room of the mission style winery.

With its international reach and long standing tradition in the evolution of Mexican wines, Domecq is more commercial than many of the boutique wineries you will find in the area. The winery offers tours in English and Spanish and some of the most reasonably priced tasting in the entire valley. The tours are free of charge.

Casa Pedro Domecq, km 73 Carretera Federal #3 Tecaté - Ensenada, Phone: (646) 155-2249, Website: http://www.pernod-ricard-mexico.com

Accomodations

Where to stay in Valle De Guadalupe

Hacienda-style hotels and rustic cabins, a Tuscan villa and safari-style tents… there's nothing ordinary about the accommodations in and around Guadalupe Valley, as cutting-edge design and creativity infuse all aspects of this wine-country paradise. But if we had to pick one hotel, which got the cross border talk started and was able to contribute at large to the success of Baja's wine region as a destination of choice for international travelers, it has to be **Encuentro Guadalupe**. With its minimalistic hillside bungalows, which allow panoramic views of the surrounding vineyards as well as a spot on marketing approach as an eco-resort, it has been written up in about every high gloss travel and lifestyle magazine.

The hotel's 20 mini lofts are set on 40 acres of gorgeous, unspoiled terrain. All rooms have minimalistic décor and floor to ceiling windows, which allow you to take in the view. You also get your very own balcony with a fire pit, perfect to enjoy a bottle of wine in the evening. There is no TV or phone, just an Ipad docking station and a walkie-talkie to communicate with the front desk. It feels a bit like a cabin in the woods. Not posh but unique and ideal for anyone who wants to get back in touch with nature but would never set a foot in a traditional cabin.

If you are looking for a more traditional accommodation, check **La Villa Del Valle**. With its six beautifully furnished suites, lavender fields, organic gardens, stylish pool scene and a lakeside deck to sip their award-winning wines, this Tuscan villa stunner is like a study in good taste. Walk the labyrinth, enjoy a yoga class, play a round of bocce or visit the spectacular eco-winery. Eileen and Phil Gregory's La Villa Del Valle is an unforgettable paradise in which you immediately will feel at ease.

Another popular option is **Adobe Guadalupe**. Because of its central location in El Porvenir, the luxury hotel offers easy access to many wineries. It's further known as a breading center for Azteca horses, allowing guests to explore the local wineries on horseback. The six bedroom suites are named after archangels, Uriel, Gabriel, Rafael, Serafiel, Kerubiel and Miguel, and designed in the same Persian style as the entire ranch.

Breakfast is served in a large communal kitchen, where you often share the table with the property's horse trainer, agronomist (seed and soil scientists) or the owners, Tru Miller, a Dutch Native, and her California based banker husband Donald.

The hotel is set among 60 acres of vineyards. The first vines were planted in 1998. Today, Adobe Guadalupe features an extensive collection of artisan wines, including Cabernet Sauvignon, Merlot, Nebbiolo, Tempranillo, Malbec, Grenache, Cinsault, Mourvedre, Syrah and wine made from Viognier grapes.

Rancho Maria Teresa, best known as the home of the **Posada Inn Hotel**, is your best bet for family friendly accommodation in the Valle De Guadalupe. The ranch offers a wide array of outdoor activities and features multiple pools, volleyball and basketball courts.

Next to the Posada Inn is the **Campestre Los Naranjos** restaurant, which serves authentic Mexican food like fajitas and enchiladas as well as locally raised quail. On the grounds you will further find two wineries: **Vinedos de Santana** and **Hacienda La Cava Boutique**, where you can sample Cabernet Sauvignon, Merlot and Barbera artisan wine, which are all produced locally on the ranch.

A more recent addition is the hotel **Cabanas Cuatro Cuatros**, which is best described as a cluster of fourteen large tents nestled within vineyards and mountains overlooking the ocean. The atmosphere is rural just like you picture it when heading out for a weekend in the woods. But unlike traditional camping, a stay at Cabanas Cuatro Cuatros comes without the headache of having to share community showers. There is also no walk to a bathroom a mile down the road. This luxury tent settlement at the western tip of the Baja wine country is chock full of cosmopolitan features such as a spa, air conditioning, mini bars and luxury beds. It's like camping without the aches and pains of spending the night on a yoga mat. Cabanas Cuatro Cuatros is perfect for for everyone who digs the outdoors but has long outgrown a traditional tent.

Encuentro Guadalupe, km 75 Carretera Federal #3 Tecaté - Ensenada, Phone: (646) 155-2775, Website: http://antiresorts.com

La Villa Del Valle, Rancho San Marcos Toros Pintos S/N, Francisco Zarco, Phone: (646) 156-8007, Website: http://www.lavilladelvalle.com

Adobe Guadalupe, Parcela A-1 S/N, El Porvenir, Phone: (646) 155-2094, Website: http://adobeguadalupe.com

Posada Inn Hotel, km 82.5 Carretera Federal #3 Tecaté - Ensenada, Phone: (646) 155- 2450, Website: http://www.ranchomariateresa.com/rooms.html

Cabanas Cuatro Cuatros, km 89 Carretera Federal #3 Tecaté - Ensenada,

.

Paralelo

Used tires, refurbished gasoline tanks etc… Paralelo takes recycling to new heights. The winery was designed by the renown architect Alejandro D'Acosta and his wife, Claudia Turrent. The couple speaks of their style as "revolución verde", the "green revolution".

The Valle De Guadalupe has been the testing ground for their sustainable way of living philosophy, which they adopted from the indigenous people of Oaxaca. The couple volunteered in the region and built health facilities as well as cultural centers before introducing their vernacular architecture to the Baja wine country. The architectural approach is completely based on materials that surround them. You work with what's at hand. And, south of the border, that's often "basura", "trash", as Acosta doesn't hesitate to point out.

During harvest time, visitors can witness trucks driving up the winery's eastern ramp to the corrugated metal roof, which is painted in the color of nearby olive trees, before releasing grapes into the vats below. Wide walls, punctuated with barrel-shaped windows on each side of the building, regulate the airflow. There are no pumps and no electricity is used for cooling. Everything at Paralelo is run by gravity.

The idea behind the wine making process is as ambitious as the architectural design. Paralelo is owned by Alejandro's brother, the acclaimed wine maker Hugo D'Acosta, and set on 250 acres of carefully tended Barbera, Cabernet Sauvignon, Petite Sirah, Merlot, Sauvignon Blanc, Syrah and Zinfandel vines. During production, the grapes are intentionally mixed. That means: Paralelo uses identical ingredients, in exact proportions, yet nurtured on different terrain, allowing the same grape varietal giving forth a complex and unique flavor from its twin, depending on whether it has flourished in sandy earth, rocky ground, hillside or reddish clay.

Needless to say, Hugo D'Acosto is considered the visionary among Baja's winemakers, a wine genius, renowned both in Mexico and internationally. But that doesn't mean he's afraid to pass on his knowledge. Besides Paralelo, Hugo D'Acosta is also the force behind the winery and tasting room **Casa de Piedra** and the head of **La Escuelita**, the local non-profit winemaking school.

Paralelo, km 73.5 Carretera Federal #3 Tecaté – Ensenada, Phone: (646) 156-5267, Website: www.paralelo.com.mx

Viñedos Lafarga

One of the newer wineries in Valle De Guadalupe, the story of Viñedos Lafarga dates back to the mid-1990s, when the three brothers Abel, Bernardo and Roberto Lafarga purchased several hectares of land in the region. They planted four distinctive grape varietals: Cabernet Sauvignon, Merlot, Nebbiolo and Syrah and released their first label wine at the annual Valle de Guadalupe harvest festival, Fiesta de la Vendimia, in 2004. The release was well received and quickly earned the Lafarga winery acceptance as one of the bright new stars of the acclaimed Ruta del Vino in Baja California.

Lafarga has two vineyard locations, one at the eastern end of the valley and one just north of San Antonio De Las Minas, about halfway between the northern and southern arm of the wine route and accessible from both highways. They bring forth 1,000 cases of wine annually with an ultimate production goal of 5,000 cases. Of particular interest are the Esther and Don Jose 1905 wines, which were developed by the brothers in honor of their parents.

The wines are offered for purchase at **Cava de Esquina** in Ensenada and also at **La Contra**. A wine-making and tasting facility in the Valle De Guadalupe is in the process of being constructed.

Viñedos Lafarga, km 78 & km. 95.5 Carretera Federal #3 Tecaté – Ensenada, Phone: (646) 189-6070, (646)178-6755, (646) 178-7060, Website: www.lafargavin.com

Fancisco Zarco Area & the Southern Valle De Guadalupe
Lechuza Vinicola

Reminiscent of the early Napa days, Lechuza Vinicola is a boutique winery you can't help but fall in love with. It was established in 2005 by Ray and Patty Magnussen after enjoying numerous vacations in the area. Only two years later, the couple released their first vintage.

Today, Lechuza Vinicola offers a Cabernet Sauvignon, Nebbiolo, Merlot, Tempranillo and Grenache Rose.

Tours and tastings at Lechuza Vinicola are by appointment only. All tours are private and offer an in-depth look into the world of grape growing.

While working on your buzz in the cellar during the accompanying tasting, the outdoor kitchen whips up a custom menu. Does it get any better?

Lechuza Vinicola, km 82.5 Carretera Federal #3 Tecaté – Ensenada, Phone: (646)947-6315, Website: www.vinoslechuza.com

Mogor Badan

Mogor Badan is a rustic, family-owned farm and winery, which was founded in 1952 by a Swiss couple, Henri Badan and Clotilde Dangon. Initially, the couple sold its grapes to large wineries in the area, but, eventually, the two started working on their own batch.

It wasn't until their son, Antoine Badan, started producing the rather exotic Chasselas though, a white wine variety mostly identified with the cool-climate in Switzerland, that the winery, which works under the El Mogor label, made itself a name in the area. The crisp, fruity and sparkling Chasselas wine is quite rare in Mexico and Antoine Badan had the distinction of being the only producer in Valle de Guadalupe working with the varietal.

Today, Antoine Badan's sister, Natalia Badan, is in charge of the estate. Raised on her parents' farm, the deep passion she developed for the environment and local agriculture has made her one of the most high-profile organic growers in the region. Instead of using underground irrigation pipes, the Mogor Badan winery and farm collects water from the mountains. "I have very little water," Natalia Badan often explains to the interested visitors. "But it is extremely good" and contributes to the wines being free of saltiness.

At the weekly farmer's market Natalia Badan shares her love for organic produce. The market is open Wednesdays and Saturdays and features farm-produced fruits and vegetables as well as honey and Natalia's famous homemade bread and sauces. Natalia Badan is well known within the entire Guadalupe Valley for her recipes such as empanadas, which are filled with locally made cheeses and homegrown herbs.

Editor's Pick: Deckman's en el Mogor

Located in the middle of the Mogor Badan vineyard is the restaurant Deckman's en el Mogor. It's run by Drew Deckman, an American-born chef who can usually be found behind the stove, set under a grove of trees and surrounded by a casual grouping of chairs.

Drew Deckman calls his restaurant an "anti-restaurant" and that's a pretty striking way to describe it. It feels like a few seats were pulled out of the farmhouse to host unexpected guests. But that's the very reason you will feel at home here from the very minute you set a foot on the property.

Mogor Badan, km. 85.5 Carretera Federal #3 Tecaté – Ensenada, Phone: (646) 188-3960, Website: http://deckmans.com

Viñas De Garza

Built on a ridge with a commanding view of the southern part of the valley, Viñas De Garza is a hidden gem. Most visitors discover the winery when venturing off the beaten path, just to find themselves returning for many more visits. It's the serenity that draws you in and the family friendly atmosphere is what makes you want to stay. In other words: it's difficult not to fall in love with the oasis Amado Garza and his wife have built on this stunning 3-hectares track of land neighboring San Antonio De Las Minas.

The couple purchased the vineyard only a little over 10 years ago but already produces a total of 9 labels. The outside wine tasting bar is located on a charming wooden deck with views overlooking the beautifully manicured vineyards and bountiful bougainvillea. Wine tastings often come with a private tour by the owner. Viñas De Garza is really difficult to beat!

Vinas De Garza, km. 87 Carretera Federal #3 Tecaté – Ensenada, Phone: (646)175-8883, Website: http://www.vinosdegarza.com

Sol Y Barro

Located past Viñas De Garza, a little further down the dirt road, are the wine cellars of the ranch Sol Y Barro. As the name suggests, the winery is built solely out of clay with wondrous curving walls painted in soft colors.

The Swiss born owner and designer, Aime Desponds, became fascinated with this unusual form of design when attending a workshop led by Linda and Ianto Evans in 2003. Desponds vowed that one day he would create his own house out of clay. Two years later, he purchased a tract of land neighboring his cousins' Mogor Badan farm, located about halfway between Francisco Zarco and San Antonio De Las Minas, and went to work on his dream. It only took one year for the clay house and the adjacent cellars to be completed. The "green" design of the winery allows for natural air circulation to be used as a cooling system.

The wine production turned out to be a huge success for the Swiss designer. Desponds dry-farms Grenache grapes and blends them with a touch of Cabernet Sauvignon as well as a splash of Petite Sirah, producing a limited yearly run of one of the most acclaimed artisan wines in all of Mexico. Called Sol Y Tierra, the delicious blend embodies much of what makes the Valle de Guadalupe so special. It has been heralded as "stunning" by Mexican wine expert Steve Dryden who called Desponds a "wizard".

Sol Y Barro, km. 87 Carretera Federal #3 Tecaté – Ensenada, Phone: (646) 155-3254

Vinacola Tres Mujeres & El Pinar De Tres Mujeres

As the name indicates, Tres Mujeres, The Three Women, is owned by three female wine entrepreneurs: Ivette Vaillard, an oceanographer and ceramist, Eva Cotero, a scientist and photographer, and Laura Macgregor, the businesswoman among the three with a degree in business administration. The women first met at Hugo D'Acosta's acclaimed wine school, which is affectionately called "La Escuelita", "The Little School". In 2003, they started Vinacola Tres Mujeres, never guessing that it would quickly turn into one of the most popular artisanal wineries in the Valle De Guadalupe.

Producing a little over 4,000 bottles a year, Vinacola Tres Mujeres is shying away from complex distribution systems. Every single bottle of wine is handcrafted, signed by the winemakers themselves and sold directly to the many visitors who arrive at the winery each week to take a tour or experience a tasting. Most of the guests have been referred by friends, and that's just the way the owners had intended it when they started Tres Mujeres. A "labor of love" project, they like to keep things personal.

Like many of the artisanal wineries in the valley, Tres Mujeres is known for its blends. Working with beloved Grenache vines that are over 30 years old, Ivette produces vintage wines tastefully experimenting not only with Grenache but also with Cabernet Sauvignon and Terrazas. She further created a memorable combination of Zinfandel, Mision and Rosa del Peru.

Eva's Merlot called "Isme" has developed a serious following among wine lovers. And Laura offers a sensational Tempranillo as well as a 100% Cabernet Sauvignon considered so good it has been called a "steal" at $20.

All Tres Mujeres wines are stored underground in the winery's new and expanded cava. The original Tres Mujeres wine cellar has been converted into a tasting room. The room is full of mosaics and ceramics, often featuring pieces of local artists. It feels a bit as if you are walking into your childhood's fairytale home.

In addition to the beloved winery, the adjacent, environmentally-friendly farm, which is part of the same property, produces a variety of hand-crafted artisanal products including olives and oil, homemade sauces and jams.

Located on the grounds of Vinicola Tres Mujeres is further the seasonal outdoor restaurant, **El Pinar de 3 Mujeres**.

Tres Mujeres, km. 87 Carretera Federal #3 Tecaté – Ensenada, Phone: (646) 173-4536

San Antonio De Las Minas

Viña de Liceaga

When you drive up the long gravel driveway leading to Viña de Liceaga, you will feel like you are entering a fairytale land. The road is flanked with majestic oak trees, some of which are some 500 years old.

Once called Rancho el Paricutin, the beautiful ranch property, which was purchased by Eduardo Liceaga Campos and is wife in 1983, is producing over 4000 cases of wine yearly, all well recognized throughout Mexico and beyond. In 2002, the winery was honored at the prestigious San Francisco International Wine Competition with the title "Best of the Nation".

Liceaga also has the distinction of being the sole winery to create and sell its own Grappa in all of Mexico. Called Aqua de Vid, the distilled spirit is made from fermented, pressed black grape pomace and aged for three years in American oak barrels.

The on-site outdoor restaurant offers simple but delicious snacks, including grilled meats, out-of-this-world tacos and handmade flour tortillas on the weekends.

Viña de Liceaga, *km. 93 , Carretera Federal #3 Tecaté-Ensenada, Phone: (646) 155-3281, Website: http://www.vinosliceaga.com*

Casa de Piedra

Casa de Piedra is the original outpost of acclaimed Mexican wine maker, Hugo D'Acosta. D'Acosta trained in France, then came to work for Santo Tomas in the 1990s, before setting up his own winery in the Guadalupe Valley.

His name is closely associated with the re-birth of the region. D'Acosta released his first vintage in 1997 and is generally referred to as the winemaker who paved the way for a new generation of independent growers with a more experimental outlook on the winemaking process. His wines, such as Vino de Piedra, a blend of Tempranillo and Cabernet Sauvignon, enjoy a cult-like status among Mexican oenophiles.

Built with recycled materials, the rust-colored Casa De Piedra is surrounded by vines, making it blend seamlessly into the landscape. If you are among the lucky few who can score a reservation for a tasting, you'll also get a tour of the facility, which has set the standard for the boutique wineries in the region.

Casa de Piedra, km. 93.5, Carretera Federal #3 Tecaté-Ensenada, Phone: (646)155-3102, Website: http://www.vinoscasadepiedra.com

Vinacola Tres Valles

Although still a relatively young winery with the first batch released exclusively among friends in the early 2000s, Vinacola Tres Valles has already received rave reviews for its wines.

The winery's aging cave and tasting room are located at the outskirts of San Antonio De Las Minas, the first large town you reach when entering the wine route from Ensenada. But winemakers work closely with growers in all three Baja valleys, Valle de Guadalupe, San Antonio de las Minas and San Vicente de Ferrer, hence the name.

Currently, Vinacola Tres Valles produces a total of 25,000 bottles. All wines are named after the local indigenous people of northern Baja California, the Kiliwa.

Vinacola Tres Valles, between km. 93 and km. 94 Carretera Federal #3 Tecaté – Ensenada (make a right at the only stop light in San Antonio de las Minas, Benito Juarez Street, then follow the signs to the winery), Phone: (646) 178-8052, Website: http://www.vinostresvalles.com

Vinisterra

Long before Guillermo Rodrigues started his first commercial wine enterprise, he used to spend summers in San Antonio de Las Minas, often inviting over friends to play dominos. It was during these summer vacations that he started to blend wines.

At first, Guillermo Rodrigues would share his wines only with friends. But it didn't take long for his hobby to outgrow the small kitchen of his summer home.

In the year 2000, Guillermo Rodriguez founded Vinisterra. In honor of the fun times with friends, he named his first label Chateau Domino.

One of the friends Guillermo Rodriguez used to play dominos with was the Swiss enologist, Christoph Gartner. But Gartner and Rodrigues didn't only share a love for the board game; they also agreed on the large potential of Mexican wines and decided to partner up. Today, Christoph Gartner handcrafts all wines and oversees the vineyards at Vinesterra.

The winery currently produces more than 7000 cases of wine each year. There are three main labels: Domino, Macouzet and Cascabel/Pedregal.

Vinisterra, between km. 93 and km. 94 Carretera Federal #3 Tecaté – Ensenada (make a right at the only stop light in San Antonio de las Minas, Benito Juarez Street, then follow the signs to the winery), Phone: (646) 178-3310 or (646) 178-3350, Website: http://www.vinisterra.com

Santo Tomas

After Jesuit priests started cultivating vines in the Valle de Guadalupe in the 18th century, Bodegas de Santo Tomas was the first commercial winery; it opened in 1888. Today, Santo Tomas is one of the largest and most well-know wineries in the area, with not one but two satellite locations in Valle De Guadalupe as well as a beloved tasting room in Ensenada.

The winery's mother facility is located at the outskirts of San Antonio De Las Minas. It's a chic and modern facility. Elegant furniture, artisanal pottery and striking pieces of art fill the premises; it feels like you are tasting wine in an art gallery.

The tasting bar itself is comprised from a repurposed olive oil press. The wine bottles waiting in the 50-foot rack decorating the walls of the room are illuminated by their own jewel-toned wrappers, flashing brilliantly against its classic dark wood. It's very stylish if not to say almost magical.

When taking the tour, note the winery's fermenting tanks that double as chalkboards, listing the types of grape, their leaf patterns, wine processes etc. There's also a video presentation and wine-specific laser show at Santo Tomas.

Santo Tomas, km. 95 Carretera Federal #3 Tecaté – Ensenada, just west of the only gas station on the wine route, Phone: (646) 178-3333, Website: http://santo-tomas.com

El Sauzal & the Western Valle De Guadalupe

Cavas Valmar

The story of Cavas Valmar began in 1919. That's the year French-man Don Federico Valentin arrived in Ensenada and started his vineyard. At first, he only produced wine for visiting friends. But that was before his two sons, Hector and Gontran Valentin, decided to sell their father's wine in the ranch's parking lot.

Back then, the family business didn't consist of much more than a small mill, a manual cork machine, a four-bottling facility, a basket press machine and 6 barrels. But after partnering up with winemak-er and Valle De Guadalupe local, Fernando Martain, Cavas Valmar expanded its production and is now crafting three varietals, Tem-pranillo, Chenin Blanc and Cabernet Sauvignon. The wines enjoy a great reputation, which reaches far beyond Mexico. In fact, Cavas Valmar is one of only a few businesses in Guadalupe Valley export-ing to the United States and Europe.

Cavas Valmar is one of the oldest wineries in the Valle De Guada-lupe. Their vineyards are located just outside of Ensenada, in Sau-zal, at the western end of the wine country.

There's also a tasting room in the town of Ensenada, which is pop-ular among visitors who want to get a taste of Mexican wines but don't have the time to make the drive to Guadalupe Valley.

Cavas Valmar, Location: Riveroll 1950, Zona Centro, 22800 Ensenada, Phone: (646)178-6405, Website: www.vinosvalmar.com

Relieve Vinicola & Mixtura

Relieve Vinicola is the first winery you will reach when entering Valle de Guadalupe on the northern route from Highway 1. The vineyard belongs to the Santos family.

Having been Ensenada locals for many generations, Wenceslao Martinez Santos purchased the 8 hectares of land at the western tip of the Baja wine country in 2004 to embrace the region's century old tradition of winemaking and invest in the growth of the valley. The winery is now run by his sons.

Besides their Tempranillo, Nebbiolo, Merlot, Malbec, Cabernet, Syrah and Pinot Noir, the Relieve Vinincola vineyards are best known as the home of the restaurant **Mixtura**. One of the newer additions at Valle de Guadalupe, the restaurant differs from the others as the food is heavily inspired by the Peruvian Cuisine.

Mixtura is an outdoor restaurant with a shipping container serving as a kitchen and only open during the summer.

Relieve Vinicola / Mixtura, Location: Granate S/N, Phone: (646) 178-6650 (Winery), (646) 132-9935 (Restaurant), Website: http://www.relieve-vinicola.com (Winery), http://www.mixtura.com.mx (Restaurant)

AlXimia

Started by a mathematician turned winemaker, the AlXimia vineyards are located on the road to El Tigre. Although not one of the main roads, the winery is difficult to miss, as it's accommodated in one of the valley's most unique buildings. Described as the "flying saucer that landed in the Valle de Guadalupe", the winery looks a lot like a space ship.

The main building features a curved roof, which is designed to collect rain for water recycling purposes. Electricity at the AlXimia vineyards is produced by solar panels, and a gravity system carries wine through its various stages of development. The entire wine making process can be observed from the second floor tasting room.

AlXimia produced the first small batch of wine in 2005, with a limited production of 20 cases of Cabernet and Cabernet-Merlot. The winery has since expanded and taken on the local tradition of blending noble Italian and Spanish varietals, making a variety of non-traditional blends.

Asked about the name, owner Alvara Alvarez-Parilla recently explained in an interview for the eBook *Conversations With Winemakers* that the winery was named after the word "Alchemy", referring to the pseudo-science of the middle ages when "scientists" tried to turn lead into gold.

The Alvarez-Parilla family has a long tradition in Baja. Alvara Alvarez-Parilla's father came to Baja some 40 years ago. He was one of the first astronomers at the local observatory.

AlXimia, km. 3, Amino Vecinal Al Tigre, Phone: (646) 947 5256, Website: http://www.alximia.com

Vinos Pijoan

Vinos Pijoan is an intimate, family-run winery, located just a few miles west of the town of Francisco Zarco along the northern part of the wine route. Perhaps their most popular wine is Leonora, named for founder Pau Pijoan's green-eyed wife. Aged for twelve months in oak, the Leonora wine is both elegant and intense with a ruby coloring and hints of chocolate, spice and vanilla. Its tannins are described as mature and pleasant, with a long and lasting finish.

Vinos Pijoan is a "green" winery. Many earth friendly practices are tested here before being promoted throughout the valley, among them the use of swallows nests in the fight against insects. Like a growing number of wineries in the area, Vinos Pijoan also supports a policy of no herbicide use.

Tastings as well as tours of the vineyard and the cellar are offered. As it's often the case with small family run wineries, there's a pretty good chance of meeting the man himself when visiting Vinos Pijoan.

Pau Pijoan, a veterinarian by trade, started making wine as a hobby. Today, retired from his job, Vinos Pijoan produces 2,500 cases of wine on five acres.

Vinos Pijoan, km. 12.8 Highway Francisco Zarco-El Tigre, Phone: (646) 171-7179, Website: http://vinospijoan.com/english-home/

Hacienda La Lomita

La Lomita is often described as the winery that best represents Mexico's future of winemaking. It was founded in 2006 by Mexican stage-actor-turned-vintner Fernando Pérez Castro and looks a lot like a medieval castle. But as you walk through the rustic wooden doors of the fairytale building with its wrought iron portico, you will get into a modern, almost hip tasting room with a gorgeous view across the vineyards and estates of the western Guadalupe Valley. That's when you realize that at Hacienda La Lomita you didn't sign up for your average tasting experience.

With only a handful of years in operation, Hacienda La Lomita has already earned several prestigious awards. Their different varieties include Cabernet Sauvignon, Chardonnay, Grenache, Merlot and Zinfandel. The winery produces eight labels and is best known for the opposing wines they call Sacro and Pagano, which translates to "sacred" and "pagan". Sacro is a fruity Cabernet-Merlot blend and Pagano is a fiery Grenache.

Guided tours of the winery are given by Enologist Reynaldo Rodriguez himself. The tours are free of charge.

Hacienda La Lomita also features an on-site restaurant which serves wood-fired meals in an al fresco garden setting.

Hacienda La Lomita, Fraccionamiento 3 Lote 13 Camino vecinal Parcela 71, Phone: (646) 156-8459, Website: http://lomita.mx

Vena Cava

A personal favorite, Vena Cava is one of a growing number of wineries that are designated to give visitors not just a taste of fine wine but also a memorable visual experience. The brainchild of Phil Gregory and his wife Eileen who also run the B&B luxury retreat **La Ville Del Valle** with the famed restaurant **Corazon de Tierra**, the winery was built completely out of reclaimed materials such as recycled boats found at a nearby port.

Originally from Manchester, the couple had a successful career in the music industry in Los Angeles before they decamped to Mexico to try their hand at organic winemaking. Their Sauvignon Blanc and Cabernet Sauvignon is served at some of the best restaurant in Mexico, such as the much talked about Pujol in Mexico City. "Phil's idea is to make elegant, understated wines", explains Eileen, "complex but easy to drink, which complement rather than fight with food for center stage".

Vena Cava is located along a dirt road, just east of La Ville Del Valle Hotel. The winery is a bit of a trek to get to but is well worth the drive. With a manmade lake with boats, a shaded canopy for dining and sipping wine and, let's not forget, the winery's very own food truck, **Troika**, you will find a hip, almost counter-culture like vibe at Vena Cava you will immediately fall in love with.

Vena Cava, *exit north near km. 88 Carretera Federal #3 Tecaté – Ensenada, then follow the signs for La Villa del Valle, Phone: (646) 156 8053, Website: www.venacavawine.com*

Villa Montefiori

The elegant Villa Montefiori was founded in 1997 by the Paoloni family. Originally from the Le Marche region outside of Tuscany in Italy, the Paolonis planted their estate with classic Italian and French grape varietals.

Today, the Paolinis are among the most respected producers in the Valle De Guadalupe and the champions of the Nebbiolo grape, the signature wine of the region. The Nebbiolo grapes in the Valle de Guadalupe produce wine darker, heavier and bolder than in Italy, as Paolo Paoloni likes to point out.

One of the most northern wineries in the Valle De Guadalupe, Villa Monefori has a privileged location at the entrance of Valle de Guadalupe, enjoying a mild climate thanks to the sea air currents from the Pacific Ocean.

Villa Montefiori, *Parcela 26 s/n. Ejido Porvenir km 9, Phone: (646) 156-8020, Website: http://www.villamontefiori.com.mx/*

Vinos Bibayoff

Vinos Bibayoff is located on Toros Pintos, a century-old farm, that is owned and operated by brothers David and Abel Bibayoff Dalgoff, hence the name. The brothers are descendants of a group of Russian Molokan families who emigrated in the early 1900s to Valle de Guadalupe via California after being persecuted by the Russian Orthodox Church for their Christian pacifist views.

Like the Dalgoffs, many Molokan refugees were attracted to the Baja region because of its agricultural potential. After being granted permission to live in Mexico by then President Porfirio Diaz, a total of 104 Molokan families purchased land and started farming, many growing grapes for the local wine production.

Realizing that they had cultivated award winning grapes, the Bibayoff family began to experiment with their own wine production. Within only a few short years, the family developed an outstanding blend of Chenin Blanc-Colombard-Muscat. Highly regarded in prestigious wine circles, the wine has recently won numerous competitions.

Truly artisan in nature, all wine at Bibayoff is bottled and labeled by hand.

On the grounds of the Bibayoff winery, visitors will also find a small museum celebrating the Russian Molokan heritage. The winery further hosts a variety of cultural events throughout the year including banquets, music and film screenings.

Vinos Bibayoff, Toros Pintos Ranch, km. 9.5 Highway Francisco Zarco-El Tigre, Phone: (646) 176-1008

El Porvenier Area

Finca la Carrodilla

With the first production run in 2011, Finca la Carrodilla is one of the newer additions in Valle De Guadalupe. It's a passion project of the Castro Family, who also runs Lomita Vinicola Mexicana in nearby San Antonio De Las Minas, a winery which is often referred to simply as La Lomita. The self-taught winemaker Fernando Perez Castro is overseeing the efforts at both locations.

Finca la Carrodilla is the only winery in Valle De Guadalupe which has received the certified organic label. The winery has an agronomist on staff at all times to supervise the grapes and organic gardens.

Eventually farm animals are supposed to be added; the Castro family already raises honey bees.

Finca la Carrodilla is entered through a rooftop garden. The garden serves as a natural cooling system for the cellars below. The focal point of the building is a shrine to the Virgin of La Carrodilla, known as the protector of wineries.

Finca La Carrodilla, Parcela 99 Z1 P14, Ejido El Porvenir, Phone: (646) 156-8052
Lomita Vinicola Mexicana, Fraccionamento 13, San Antonio De Las Minas, Phone: (646) 156-8466, Website: http://lomita.mx

El Cielo

El Cielo was started by Gustavo Ortega and his wife Daly Negrón, both experienced hoteliers from the Riviera Maya. One of Mexico's sunniest regions, this is also where they first experimented with sustainable energy, a tradition they are very fond of and they eventually ended up introducing to the Valle De Guadalupe. Their 71-acre estate, which features 12 grape varietals, an organic garden with olive trees and a fruit plantation, offsets approximately 75 percent of its energy with a state-of-the-art-solar system.

The award winning El Cielo wines are all named after astronomers and star constellations. The most well know wine is probably Capricornius, which was named Best Chardonnay in Mexico in 2013 by La Guía Catadores. In addition, be sure to taste Orion, a flirty blend of Tempranillo and Grenache, or Perseus, a successful marriage of Nebbiolo and Sangiovese, tempered in French oak.

During the summer, the Ortegas organize concerts on the grounds of their property. Most notable is the 2015 performance of salsa artist Marc Anthony.

El Cielo, *Carretera Guadalupe – El Tigre km 7.5 , Parcela 118, Ejido el Porvenir, Phone: (646) 155-2220, Website: http://vinoselcielo.com*

Las Nubes

Las Nubes, which translates to "the Clouds", is what locals call "a newbie". The winery was founded in 2008 by enologist Victor Segura and his partners. Dedicated to producing outstanding and memorable wine at reasonable cost, Las Nubes offers wine at a discount.

Las Nubes is located only minutes from the town of El Porvenir. The winery produces 6,200 cases annually. The seven varietals include their so-called "happy girl" wine Cumulus, a blend of Grenache, Carignan and Tempranillo.

Like the beloved Culumus, all wines at Las Nubes are named after cloud formations in the Kiliwa language and known for their fruitiness as well as excellent balance of sugar and acidity.

Besides grapes, the land at Las Nubes is devoted to the production of Manzanilla olives. It's a perfect fit for a property that has a bit of a Tuscan feel, with thick stone walls and hilltop facilities painted in an okra color.

The property's silver-toned olive groves are where Las Nubes hosts *Vinedos en Flor*, the "Flowering of the Vines", an event that starts off the wine season with a fiesta filled with regional dishes and local wines.

Las Nubes, *Callejon Emiliano Zapata S/N, Ejido el Porvenir, Phone: (646) 156 8037, Website: http://vinoslasnubesbc.com*

J.C. Bravo

Centrally located in the town of El Porvenir, J.C. Bravo is one of the most easily accessible wineries in the northern part of Valle De Guadalupe. The vineyard stretches out over 20 spacious hectares and features a variety of vines as well as many fruit trees.

The J.C. Bravo winery is run by Juan Carlos Bravo and his brother Martin, two of the few real locals in Valle De Guadalupe. Juan Carolos Bravo started supplying grapes to other wineries before eventually venturing into producing his own wine.

Mentored by local wine wizard Hugo D'Acosta, the Bravo brothers dry farm their grapes, allowing the natural moisture from the sea air and the local rainfall to water the land. Similarly, they eschew pesticides by allowing the winds to keep the vines clear of rot.

In addition to wine, J.C. Bravo offers locally produced olive oil and delicious orange marmalade for sale. Juan Carlos Bravo speaks some English, his bother is even more fluent. This, along with the convenient location, makes J.C. Bravo a great first winery to visit.

Like many wineries in the area, J.C. Bravo hosts several artisanal events throughout the season, showcasing local food, artwork, live music, and of course the delicious wines of the region.

J.C. Bravo, Callejon Emiliano Zapata S/N Parcela 680, Ejido el Porvenir, Phone: (646)947-6496

Emeve

The idea for Vinícola Emeve goes back to the Mexican businessman Mario Villarreal whose daughter Laura now manages the winery. Mario Villarreal had long dreamt of creating his own wine when, in early 2000, he set his eyes on a fitting piece of land in Valle De Guadalupe. He obtained cuttings from the University of California Davis, enlisted the help of noted winemaker and enologist Reynaldo Rodriguez, an Ensenada native who received his formal training in Spain and, in 2004, set about planting his first grapes.

Only two years later, the Emeve winery released its first commercial wines, a Bordeaux blend and a Malbec-Cabernet. Aged in French and American oak barrels, the wines received acclaim from the school of enology and gastronomy at Universidad Autonoma de Baja California and almost immediately started winning awards at various competitions. One of the most meaningful compliments bestowed upon Emeve wines came from *The Good Table*, which detected notes of mango and ancho chile in the aroma of the winery's 2007 Cabernet Sauvignon, naming it a "truly Mexican wine".

Seated upon 945 acres of beautiful terrain between Francisco Zarco and El Porvenir, Vinícola Emeve features its own tasting room amid an endless sea of gorgeous vines. The wines are served with local olive snacks and cheeses.

Emeve, Camino a San José de la Zorra, Parcela 67, Ejido El Porvenir, Phone: (646) 156-8019, Website: http://vinicolaemeve.com

Barón Balch'é

The name Barón Balch'é, which means "ceremonial beverage", is meant to honor past kingdoms. "Wine invites us to share our feelings," the website of the winery proclaims. "It provokes discussion, passion and emotion!"

Barón Balch'é was the first winery in the entire Guadalupe Valley to build an underground cava, commonly referred to as a wine cellar. Within four years of breaking ground, the first 2500 cases of wine were released.

Today, Barón Balch'é produces 120,000 bottles each year through three different labels: Rincon de Barón, Barón Balch'é and Premium Balch'é. All of the wines are exclusively sold to the Mexican market, making a bottle of Barón Balch'é a popular souvenir for visitors.

The Rincon de Barón is the most reasonable priced label. It offers three fresh, lightly aged wines including Double Blanc, Chardonnay and Mexcla de Tintos. The blends are defined by their sweetness, fruity aroma and interesting colors such as the very clear and translucent golden Sauvignon Blanc.

Recently, *The SanDiegan* called Barón Balch'é a "hidden treasure". And they were not lying. The winery is difficult to spot, as it's literally buried behind an old graveyard. If you missed the sign, stop at Adobe Guadalupe. They can point the vineyard out to you; it's only one lot over.

Barón Balch'é, Ejido El Porvenir, Phone: (646) 622-5276, Website: http://baronbalche.com

Vinicola Torres Alegre

The first enologist in Mexico with a PhD in his field, Dr. Torres Alegre graduated with a degree in agricultural engineering from the National Agricultural School of Chapingo before he went on to the University of Bordeaux, France for his doctorate. During his time in France, he developed numerous innovative concepts and practices for winemaking, many of which are now not only put to use at Vinicola Torres Alegre but are widely accepted throughout the industry.

The day to day activities at Vinicola Torres Alegre are run by Dr. Torres Alegre's son, Leonardo Torres, an accomplished winemaker himself. By appointment, he guides small groups through the family winery and explains the various processes, including the winery's gravity filtration system.

Vinicola Torres Alegre is located on a dirt road that runs behind Adobe Guadalupe Vineyards and Inn. It blends so delicately into the Baja Californian landscape, that you can easily overlook it amid vineyards and olive groves. So you will have to keep your eyes open.

Vinicola Torres Alegre, *Ejido El Porvenir, Phone: (646) 176-3345, Website: http://vinicolatorresalegreyfamilia.com/blog/*

Quinta Monasterio

Quinta Monasterio is owned by the Rodriquez family. Like so many farmers in the region, Reynaldo Rodriquez Jr. and his father, Reynaldo Sr., used to grow grapes for other bottlers before taking a leap of faith and starting their own label in 2006.

Today, the family winery averages a production of 4,000 cases a year which include an apricot-peach-pear Chardonnay, a Merlot, Cabernet Franc and several red blends.

But Quinta Monasterio isn't only known for its wine. What makes this winery a truly special place and a mandatary stop on every tour of Valle De Guadalupe is the on-site spa treatment room as well as Quinta Monasterio's unique body products, which are exclusively made from grapes and wine leavings. There is even a merlot-colored "grape gravel" that crunches beneath your feet when you walk up to the spa.

All spa treatments come with lunch and wine. Do we need to say more?

Quinta Monasterio, *Road to San Jose De La Zorra, Parcela 12, Ejido El Porvenir, Phone: (646) 565-1335*

Shimul

The northernmost winery in Valle De Guadalupe, Shimul is located on the road to San Jose De La Zora. Not too many visitors make the drive up here; the estate, which is owned by the Ptacnik family, is rather secluded.

Due to the low number of visitors, you may want to call ahead of time to ensure the winery is open on the day of your visit. Advance scheduling of tastings is recommended, especially when visiting during the week.

Once you have worked your way up the winding dirt road into the foothills, you will be greeted by a neatly manicured outdoor area. Soak in the million-dollar view of the valley before heading inside. Tastings at Shimul are private and very likely to be conducted by the winemakers themselves.

Often referred to as the "the Rodeo Drive of the Guadalupe Valley", owner Alvaro Ptacnik contributes the high quality of the Shimul grapes to the special micro climate at the winery's mountain location. Tugged away, the Shimul vineyards are located at a higher altitude than most facilities in the Guadalupe Valley, allowing the grapes to grow on a granite soil. The granite, as Alvaro Ptacnik likes to point out, does not hold the water like clay, therefore stressing the vines to produce a concentration of flavor.

Shimul, Road to San Jose De La Zora, Ejido El Porvenir, Phone: (646) 177-2108, Website: http://www.shimul.net

Vinos Suenoz

Vinos Suenoz is what locals call a wine boutique. It's probably best explained as a specialty store in which you can taste and purchase wines from the Vinicola Don Juan, including their rare apple wine. None of the wines and other local products available for purchase at the store are made on site. Thus there are no tours offered. Vinos Suenoz is known for its fun tastings.

Vinos Suenoz, Calle Principal No.1., Ejido El Porvenir, Phone: (646) 179-4763

Vinos Fuentes

Situated on slightly more than 70 hectares along both sides of the riverbed, Vinos Fuentes immediately vows visitors with its retreat-style atmosphere. The property was purchased by patriarch Hector Fuentes in 1958 who raised cattle on the land and planted fruit trees. It wasn't until he retired and handed operation of the family farm over to his son, Miguel Fuentes, that this traditional Valle De Guadalupe farm was turned into a vineyard. Miguel Fuentes had a dream of turning the property into an artisan winery and, with the support of his brothers, did exactly that.

Wine production at Vinos Fuentes officially began in the year 2000. Ten different types of wine and a variety of delicious table grapes are now produced on the property. Wines offered include Cabernet Sauvignon, French Colombard, Grenache, Merlot, Muscat, Nebbiolo, Petite Sirah, Port, Tempranillo, and a handful of Cabernet blends.

Miguel Fuentes, who holds a degree from the University of California Davis in International Agricultural Development, is one of the kindest and most outgoing hosts any guest could hope for. Very passionate about wine, he oversees every aspect of the winemaking process at Vinos Fuentes and also participates in the winery's guided tours.

Please arrange tours in advance. Appointments are necessary. Reservations for tastings are not required.

Vinos Fuentes, Calle Principal No. 290, Ejido El Porvenir, Phone: (646) 155-2044,

Monte Xanic

Founded in 1987 by five friends and named for a Cora Indian word meaning "flower blooming after the first rain", Monte Xanic was one of Mexico's first boutique wineries and the first winery in the Valle De Guadalupe to fully commit to artisan winemaking. The approach included controlling the harvest yield, hand picking the grapes at night and frequent pruning of the vines.

Today, Monte Xanic produces over 50,000 cases of wine annually and is considered the star of Baja California wines, setting the standard by which all other Mexican boutique wineries are judged. A select few of the Xanic wines are even selected for export and can be found at various Whole Foods markets in the US.

The Xanic winery is perched atop an amber mountain and boasts 150 acres of vines, including popular Bordeaux and Rhône varieties as well as some Spanish, Italian and Chardonnay grapes. A private tour of the facilities reveals the largest wine cellar in Latin America, carved into and cooled by the ancient stone of the mountain. With a private lake to look out on, the setting couldn't be more serene and is difficult to match.

Monte Xanic, Calle Francisco Zarco S/N, Ejido El Porvenir, Phone: (646) 155-2080, Website: http://www.montexanic.com.mx/home-en

Chateau Camou

Located near Monte Xanic is the impressive Chateau Camou winery, which was built entirely in the late XIX mission style. The winery is located on an almost 100-acre estate called Canada del Trigo. Originally planted in the 1930s, the vineyards thrive in a box canyon and wind around two hills. It's a beautiful setting.

The winemaker at Chateau Camou is Bordeaux-trained Victor Manuel Torres. He purchased the vineyard with the goal of bringing the finest of European wine-making practices to Baja California and still consults with his French teachers and colleagues on a regular basis.

Besides tastings, Chateau Camou offers very unique behind the scenes tour, during which you follow winemaker Victor Manuel Torres around the vineyard. The tour is a must for all wine geeks.

Cateau Camou is a hidden gem. But with the following directions you should have no problem finding the winery: When heading north on the main road, Highway 3, turn left at the Health Center (IMSS Centro de Salud), then right at the end of Adobe Guadalupe's vineyards. You'll see the Chateau Camou winery on top of the hill on your left.

Chateau Camou, Ejido El Porvenir, Phone: (646) 177-2221, Website: http://www.chateau-camou.com.mx

Francisco Zarco Area

Vinedos Malagón

Vinedos Malagón sits on 400 acres of rolling hills overlooking Francisco Zarco, the most northern town on the wine route. First settled and planted with Grenache grapes in the early 1900s by Russian Molokan settlers, the vineyard has been in existence for over 100 years. It's now run by Jose Luis Malagón who gave the winery its name.

Malagón wines have been highly praised in international publications such as *Wine Spectator*. The prestigious magazine featured the winery's 2006 Reserva de Familia, an elegant blend of Cabernet-Sauvignon, Grenache, Merlot and Petite Syrah, aged for 12 months in new French oak barrels.

Pushing up even further the already high hopes for the winery is Alberto Rubio. Known in wine circles for his work with Mogor-Badan, the winemaker recently joined the team at Vinedos Malagón.

If you plan to stop at the winery for a tasting, arrange a private afternoon sitting in the old, reconstructed adobe tasting house. The tasting room features a small wine bar and kitchen, two sitting rooms furnished with rustic artisanal pieces and dual outdoor patios.

The vineyards at Vinedos Malagón also house a small bed and breakfast with 3 guest rooms, all furnished with beautifully crafted pieces made by local artisans.

Vinedos Malagòn, Calle Sexta #75, Francisco Zarco, Phone: (646) 155-2102, Website: http://www.vinedosmalagon.com

Tintos del Norte 32

After working in commercial aviation for 34 years, Captain Oscar Obregon decided to purchase land in Valle de Guadalupe and start a winery. He named the winery North Side 32 or short: 32 North, referring to the vineyard's precise geographical location.

Tintos del Norte 32 was founded in 2005 and is currently producing about 2000 cases of wine per year. One of the most popular varieties at the winery is the vintage 32 North, a Cabernet Sauvignon.

Although still in its early stages, Tintos del Norte 32 has already won a number of awards and is definitely one of the local wineries to look out for.

Tintos del Norte 32, at the end of Calle 10, Francisco Zarco, Website: http://www.vinosnorte32.com

Restaurants

The largest accumulation of restaurants in Guadalupe Valley you will find in San Antonio De Las Minas and Francisco Zarca. They include such well known establishments like **Deckman's en El Mojor** but also smaller, more hidden finds like the casual wine bar **La Goterea**.

Located about halfway between the two towns is Javier Plascenscia's **Finca Altozano**, which has fast become the go-to restaurant in the Valle de Guadalupe. And that's not only due to the culinary chef being the face of the new Baja Med Cuisine; the restaurant's setting is simply breathtaking with the entire place being out in the open and the rolling hills of the Valle de Guadalupe taking center stage. It's one of these places where - summer or winter—hours go by in minutes and daylight dims nearly unnoticed. Finca doesn't suffer a lack of seating but reservations are hard to come by. So call ahead of time to ensure a table.

Another Valle De Guadalupe icon is **Deckman's en El Mogor**. Drew Deckman is a Georgia native who trained under legendary French chefs Paul Bocuse and Jacques Maximin. While working at the restaurant Vitus in Reinstorf, he was awarded a Michelin star. Later, he served as the executive chef at the Four Seasons in Berlin. When he moved to Mexico, he did so to pursue competitive fishing. Before settling in the Guadalupe Valley full time, he spent half of the year in Cabo fishing and the other half building up his new restaurant. Not originally from Mexico, Drew Deckman has developed his own spin on the country's traditional cuisine. In an interview, which was featured in the eBook *Conversations With Winemakers*, he explained his approach, which respects the origin but takes a different road. "The best guys in Mexico", Drew Deckman likes to point out, "are doing traditional food in a way that you look at it and you wouldn't recognize that this is a traditional recipe." Besides his new spin on the country's traditional cuisine, reviewers often praise the great energy at Deckman's en El Mogor. This, at large, can be attributed to the open stove being placed a stone's throw from the tables.

A stark contrast to the vibe at Deckman's and Javier Plascenscia's Finca is the indoor restaurant **Corazon De Tierra**, which is located adjacent to La Ville del Valle. Run and co-owned by top Mexican chef Diego Hernandez, the restaurant is accommodated in one of the most modern and most architecturally forward spaces you will find in the entire Guadalupe Valley. The multicourse tasting menu changes daily, depending on what's sprouting out of the dirt just outside the restaurant's floor-to-ceiling windows. It's this thoughtful farm to table philosophy that has earned Diego Hernandez' Corazon De Tierra the top spot when it comes to the most cutting-edge cooking experience in Valle De Guadalupe. It's also what makes it worth the drive through the many potholes you will encounter on the dirt road leading to the restaurant's remote location.

More easily accessible, and just a stones throw off the highway connecting Ensenada and Tecaté, lies the hidden, rather non-descript but lovely farmhouse **Laja**. Referring to the local name for the granite bedrock found throughout the region, Laja is the Valle De Guadalupe base of Jair Téllez, who is best known as the Executive chef of MeroToro in Mexico City. Known to respect local traditions, Jair Tellez's cheerful cooking offers a tasting tour of the Baja region, starting right outside in the restaurant's prolific vegetable garden. Just like at the flagship location, you won't find white tablecloths at Laja's. Instead you will be sitting on bare-wood tables. Non-traditional crockery completes the restaurant's rustic, convivial and unpretentious offering.

For authentic Mexican breakfast stop at **La Cocina de Doña Esthela**, a local hole-in-the-wall eatery in El Porvenir. First discovered by the hungry cast and crew of a telenovela filming at the nearby Hacienda la Lomita vineyard, word of Doña Esthela's out-of-this-world breakfast dishes has spread as far as England, where the eatery was recently awarded the "Best Breakfast In The World" award by the international culinary website and mobile app *FoodieHub*.

Deckman's en El Mogor, km 85.5 Carretera Federal #3 Tecaté – Ensenada, Phone: (646)188-3960, Website: www.deckmans.com

La Goterea, km. 92 Carretera Federal #3 Tecaté – Ensenada, Phone: (646)136-6879

Corazon De Tierra, exit km 88 Carretera Federal #3 Tecaté – Ensenada, Rancho Sicomoro,
Phone: (646) 156-8030, Website: http://corazondetierra.com

Laja, km 83 Carretera Federal #3 Tecaté – Ensenada, Phone (646) 155-2556, Website: http://lajamexico.com/

La Cocina de Doña Esthela, Rancho San Marcos, Domicilio Conocido S/N, El Porvenir, Phone: (646) 156-8453

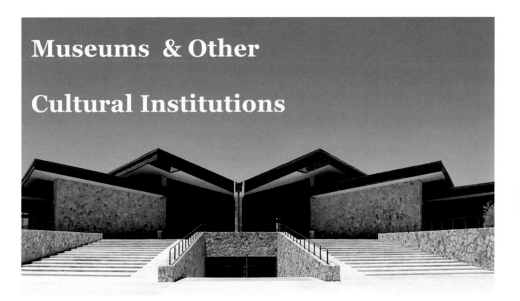

Museums & Other Cultural Institutions

Museo de la Vid y el Vino

Right across the street from Hacienda Guadalupe, in the heart of the Baja wine country, you will spot a modern, state of the art structure. Built in 2012, the structure houses the region's Wine Museum, Museo de la Vid y el Vino.

The entrance of the museum is designed as if you were walking into a wine cellar. Once you've made your way into the exhibit halls, you will find the museum to be a great place to learn not only about the early days of winemaking in Valle De Guadalupe but also about the process of turning grapes into wine. The exhibits touch on everything from soil and weather requirements to the planting of grapes to bottling. In addition, you will find a spot-on demonstration on how the wine making process in the Valle De Guadalupe has evolved over the years, making the region the poster child of the green wine movement. Or maybe you simply use the museum as a quiet and cool spot to sober up in between tours of the numerous wineries.

All exhibits are in Spanish, but if you aren't familiar with the language, the staff can arrange for a free guide who will walk you through the halls and provide you with an English translator.

In addition to its wine exhibits, the museum features rotating art displays from local artists. The art exhibits alone are often worth the visit and have received a lot of praise from visitors.

Museo de la Vid y el Vino, km 81.3 Carretera Federal #3 Tecaté – Ensenada, Opening hours: Tuesday – Sunday 9:00 AM – 5:00 PM, closed Monday, Admission: 50 Pesos, Phone: (646) 156-8165, Website: www. museodelvinobc.com

La Escuelita

Located in the town of El Porvenir is La Escuelita, or "the Little School". Mexico's wine guru Hugo d'Acosta started the educational center in 2004. Its official name is Union de Productores del Valle de Guadalupe de RL de CV or Estacion de Oficios del Porvenir. But if you call it by its official name, most likely nobody will know what you are talking about, as it's commonly referred to as La Escuelita.

La Escuelita is managed by Thomas Egli, a swiss enologist, who hand-selects a few aspiring winemakers for his class every year. The school focuses on developing unique wine brands and has thus made a large contribution to the success of the Baja wine region.

The "wine class" is held in August. It usually comprises of about 25 students, most of them with some Spanish-language knowledge. At a cost of approximately $100, the aspiring winemakers receive instructions on how to use standard equipment and get a hands-on experience in working with grapes, learning both traditional techniques as well as the use of more modern technology.

Some of Baja's top winemakers count themselves as graduates of La Escuelita, including Phil Gregory from Vena Cava, Joaquin Prieto from Tres Valles, Pau Pijoan from Vinas Pijoan, Roberto Lafarga from Vinos Lafarga and Eva Gotero, Yvette Vaillard and Laura MacGregor from Tres Mujeres. The wines of the most recent graduates are usually showcased during the famed Vendimia harvest festival.

The school itself is a complex of sheds and corrugated iron buildings, immediately noticeable for the great mural by local artist Carlos de la Torre painted on the side of a building. The mural shows workers dumping grapes into crushers. There is also a wall created from old wine bottles at La Escuelita.

Tours of La Escuelita are by appointment only. Call ahead of time to schedule your visit.

La Escuelita, Secundaria Tecnica #11, El Porvenir, Phone: (646) 156-5267

Off the Beaten Path: Rancho Cortes

Rancho Cortes easily flies under the radar because of its unpolished appearances. But it's one of the most famous places in the area among those in the know and not to be missed when visiting Valle De Guadalupe.

Rancho Cortes is a working ranch, best known for its grass-fed beef and lamb, its artisanal cheese and its olive oil. Farmers from all over Baja bring their olives to be pressed and turned into oil under the ranch's brand Misiones de Baja California. The smooth olive oil has garnered a cult following.

Rancho Cortez's beef and lamb is not only a favorite of Jair Téllez at the local Laja, it's also served at high-end restaurants as far as Mexico City. And if you've been to a winery in the valley that serves cheese as an appetizer, chances are it came from Rancho Cortes.

Rancho Cortes is open to visitors. And while you can experience their goods throughout the Valle De Guadalupe without going to the ranch itself, a trip is still worth it for the experience. You can observe the ranchers making cheese and peek into the ranch's cheese cave, where the wheels are being aged.

There's also a small and modest tasting room on the premises, where you can try and purchase cheese. It's a nice stop that is off the beaten path and the delicious cheeses and olive oil make it well worth the trip.

The turnoff for Rancho Cortes is located off of the road to El Porvenir, just outside of town. Simply follow the signs saying "queso", "cheese".

Off the Beaten Path: San Antonio Necua

With tourism flourishing, it's easy to forget that Valle De Guadalupe is Indian country. For easy access to one of the communities, head to San Antonio Necua. It's located near the eastern end of the valley. When turning off the main road, Highway 3, to reach the Doña Lupe winery, simply keep on driving past the vineyard. You will see signs for "Ecoturismo Kumiai".

San Antonio Necua, is one of Baja California's four Kumeyaay communities. Approximately 200 people live here. Besides a museum, a gift shop, restaurants and an outdoor amphitheater, you can also find a replica of a traditional Kumeyaay shelter in San Antonio Necua.

One of the last natural, undeveloped areas of the Guadalupe Valley, San Antonio Necua is a vivid reminder of the peninsula's original indigenous inhabitants. According to the Seminario de Historia de Baja California and the Instituto de Culturas Nativas de Baja California (also known as CUNA), there are roughly 2,000 members of the Pai-Pai, Kumeyaay, Cucapá and Kiliwa tribes remaining in northern Baja.

If we overlooked your winery, we apologize. Please send us a quick note. We will be sure to include you in the next edition. All our books are work in progress and updated on a consistent basis.

Email: info@hauserpub.com

Disclaimer

Travel information can change unexpectedly and quickly. We strongly recommend you confirm all details, including opening hours and prices, before visiting any of the attractions listed. While we ensure that the information is up-to-date at the time of publishing, we make no representations or warranties with respect to the accuracy or completeness of the content; all the information is subject to change without notice. We further disclaim all warranties, including without limitation warranties of fitness for a particular purpose and accept no responsibility or liability of any kind. The listing of an attraction, organization, company or website in this book is solely for the purpose of information; we do not endorse them or the information they provide. Neither the publisher nor the author shall be liable for any damages that may result in participating in sightseeing opportunities or any activities described in this book.

Hauser
Publishing

Made in the USA
San Bernardino, CA
27 December 2018